ONE PERCENT BETTER

A STORY ABOUT HOW TO CLOSE THE GAP
FROM WHERE YOU ARE
TO WHERE YOU WANT TO BE

BRIAN CAIN, MPM

#1 International Best-Selling Author

PRAISE FOR *ONE PERCENT BETTER*

"*One Percent Better* should be required reading for anyone wanting to become the best version of themselves. The principles taught in this book I applied on a daily basis when I was a Navy SEAL and Navy SEAL Instructor. I also apply these same principles now as a father and business owner. If you want to succeed at anything, it all starts with creating your one percent better 14:24 intentional game plan."

Sean Haggerty, MPM
Former US Navy SEAL & US Navy SEAL Instructor
CEO, Protector Brewery
San Diego's First and Only Organic Brewery

"As a mixed martial arts fighter and former multi-division MMA Champion who lost his first title fight and lost his first title defense fight, you learn that being intentional and moving from a mindset of preference to a mindset of principle makes all the difference. Brian Cain was my mental performance coach, and in this book, he shares everything we worked on that helped me to become the fighter I was in my career by simply working to get one percent better on my mental game."

Georges St-Pierre
13x Ultimate Fighting Championship
Mixed Martial Arts World Champion

"A must-read for any teacher or leader."

Shane Backlund
Superintendent
Selah School District, Selah, WA

"Another gem by Cain. This book will change the way you look at self-development and growth."

Eric Davis, MPM
Middle School Principal
Chief Joseph Middle School, Richland, WA

"Brian Cain has done it again. *One Percent Better* is such a simple and powerful concept. I will be sharing this with my students every year."

Dr. Rob Gilbert
Professor of Sport Psychology
Montclair State University
Creator of the Success Hotline Podcast

"Brian was so impactful as our opening day speaker that we asked him to come back for a second year in a row. This book and the principles contained within it sustained motivation and professional development in our staff like I have never seen in my 30+ years in public education. This book really helps you move from temporary to legendary and gives you a game plan to re-energize and stay motivated every day."

Ann Cardon
Superintendent
St. Joseph Public Schools, St. Joseph, Michigan

"My favorite book ever."

Tom Mietus, MPM
Athletic Director
Glenbrook South High School, Glenbrook, IL

Brian Cain, MPM
Brian Cain Peak Performance, LLC

One Percent Better
A Story about How to Close the Gap
From Where You Are to Where You Want to Be

©2022 by Brian Cain, MPM

Printed in the United States of America
Edited by: Mary Lou Reynolds

INTRODUCTION

Joe Bigelow, aka "Mr. Big," is a 20+ year veteran teacher in the St. Joseph School District. Mr. Big was hired right out of his undergraduate degree program and has been at the same school ever since. Year by year his motivation, connection, and performance in the classroom and in life are dwindling.

Sundra "Sunny" Torina has worked in the cafeterias of the St. Joseph School District for over 40 years and is beloved by everyone in the district. Her positive energy, attitude, and connection have had a positive impact on everyone in the school district, except for Mr. Big.

Mr. Big is at a crossroads in life. He's been put on a professional development plan at school by his principal, Mr. Weston, and on a personal development plan at home by his wife Erin.

With the new school year starting tomorrow with day one of yet another in-service training, Mr. Big has an uneasy feeling in his stomach, knowing that his 'here we go again' mentality isn't helping his current situation, lack of motivation, inability to connect and his subpar performance. The problem is, he doesn't know what to do to find the passion, energy, and enthusiasm he had in his first few years of teaching and marriage.

—

7

As he switches off the lamp next to his bed and lays his head back onto the pillow, he can't help but think, *'This year, something HAS to be different'. Something has to change.* He's just not sure what that "something" is, nor does he want to truly admit that what needs to change the most is him, his mindset, his attitude and his behavior.

CHAPTER 1
The Opportunity Clock

Beep... Beep... Beep...

It was the sound I had been dreading.

Another summer had passed by. I laid in bed wondering where all the time had gone.

"You going to seize that opportunity, Joe?" Erin asked. "Joe, your alarm!!!"

As Erin shook me in bed to remind me that my alarm was going off, I realized another school year was upon me.

Erin always referred to my alarm clock as an "opportunity clock" because she said that every day in education was an opportunity to have a positive impact on the lives of others and an opportunity to take a step towards the optimal version of you. She was the most positive person I had ever met.

We met in college, having both been education majors, and we were fortunate to get jobs in the St. Joseph school district in the same year. She taught at the elementary school and I taught in the high school.

We *had* both been so similar in our enthusiasm, energy, and purpose coming out of college. "Had"

9

is the important word there. Now, 20+ years later, we continued to drift apart. The echo of who we were yesterday was fading a bit more with each passing day.

"Joe, it's Day One. I am heading in. How can you just lie there like that? Day One is my favorite day of the year! It's the day you get to set the tone for your year," Erin said, fully dressed and about to head out the door. "I'll see you after school today."

She routinely heads out the door to get to school early. She loves to be the first one there and the last one to leave. She was called to teach. On this day, I felt like I was called to sleep.

As I pulled myself out of the sheets and sat up in bed, I thought to myself... *Here we go again. Another 180 school days till summer.*

I turned off my "opportunity clock" and took a shower, thinking about all of opportunities I was going to miss now that summer was over. Oh, how fast it had gone.

CHAPTER 2
Here We Go Again

On the drive to school I could feel my stomach toss and turn.

Another 180 school days... Geez... I thought to myself.

As I pulled into the parking lot, I found my typical routine spot near the exit. As one of the last people to pull in every day, I usually had the pick of the last spot available. I'd timed it well so that Mr. Mason, our head custodian who was as routine as they come, would finish doing his morning drive around the parking lot and would pick me up in his golf cart and drive up the hill to the school so that I didn't have to walk all that way. I didn't mind walking to my car *after* school; after all, it was all downhill.

"Here we go again, Mr. Big," Mr. Mason said to me.

"Here we go again. 180 more school days till summer," I said as I shook my head, thinking about how much more I'd like to be out on the golf course instead of walking into school for another in-service.

CHAPTER 3
Typical In-Service

The first day of in-service was just what I had expected: curriculum and instruction meetings, hours of PowerPoint presentations, updates on the negotiations between the board and teachers' union, handshakes and hot dogs at the annual welcome back BBQ lunch.

Finally, our principal, Mr. Weston, let us go back to our rooms to get set up.

Mr. Weston put me on a professional development plan last school year at our end-of-the-year teacher evaluation meeting. He said I was too negative, not enthusiastic enough, not connecting with students enough and entrenched. Although part of me agreed with him, I was still bitter every time I saw him. I guess sometimes the truth hurts.

Who is he to tell me how to teach and put me on a professional development plan? I've been doing this for 20+ years, I thought each time he'd look at me.

Finally, back in my room I printed the numbers 1-180 and hung them up on the wall as I had done for each of the last few years. I thought this was a great reminder for me and my students of how many days we had left in the school year. The countdown made it less painful.

I glanced up at the clock and noticed that it was 3:30 p.m. Contractually, we were supposed to be at school until 4:00 p.m. I quickly packed up my bag and headed to the door. It was Day One; nobody would care if I ducked out a little early, as usual. After all, creating routine is an essential part of the learning process, and my routine is showing up as late as I can and leaving as early as I can.

CHAPTER 4
What Happened?

I began the quarter mile or so walk downhill to my car and when I got there, I couldn't believe what I saw.

My tires were flat, my windows were broken, and the inside of my car looked like a swimming pool.

Someone had run a hose from the softball field all the way to my car, put it into my car through one of the broken windows, and had turned it on.

As my heart rate spiked and my adrenaline went through the roof, I slammed my bag to the ground and screamed.

CHAPTER 5
Water Buggied?

I couldn't believe it. I had parked in that spot for years and nothing like this had ever happened before.

Some kids must have been playing softball during the day and thought it would be funny to slash a car's tires, smash the windows, and fill it up with water. I had never heard of this happening.

When I called Erin to tell her what had happened, she laughed.

"You got water buggied. Are you okay?" she asked.

I replied, "Yes, I'm fine, but what do you mean by water buggied?"

"You should pay more attention to the news, Joe. People have been getting water buggied all summer around St. Joseph. There is a group of kids, kind of like a gang, that goes around and does what they did to you. They call it 'water bugging.' You just got buggied, Joe.

"Call the police and the insurance company and then call Uber. I'll see you at the house. I have a lot more work to do here since it's only Day One," Erin replied.

I called the police, called my insurance company, and took an Uber home, all the while thinking to myself, *here we go again. Another great start to another great year... Oh well... only 179 more school days to go.*

CHAPTER 6
Now What?

When Erin got home that night, she asked me how I was planning to get to school the next day. I hadn't thought about that yet; I was still thinking about who could have buggied me.

The insurance company said vandalism wasn't covered with a free rental car. It would take a few weeks to get my car assessed and fixed or deemed totaled, and for a check to be sent my way for a new car or for the repairs.

Regardless, Erin and I were now down to one car and I needed to figure out how I was going to get to school tomorrow.

"Why don't you go in with me, Joe?" she suggested.

"You leave at 6:00 a.m. and I don't have to leave till 8:00 a.m. to get to school in time, that's why," I said.

"Joe, school starts at 8:20 a.m. It takes 15 minutes to get to school and contractually we are supposed to be there from 8:00 a.m. to 4:00 p.m. Do you leave the house at 8:00?" She was shocked at what time I left since she was always out of the house before I even woke up.

"Joe, you aren't the same person I fell in love with in college and married here in St. Joseph 18 years ago. You've changed." The tone of frustration and negativity in her voice was evident.

"You know, Joe, one of the big things on your professional development plan with Mr. Weston and your personal development plan with me as your wife was to start waking up earlier and taking your job more seriously. You are a teacher, for heaven's sake. It's the most prestigious position a professional can have. You get to shape and mold the minds of youth, the future of our world, and you can't get yourself together enough to show up on time or put in a full day. Who have you become? Your only routine is to have no routine. You've become an energy sucker and I'm tired of it.

"Look, I don't want to pay for an Uber to bring you to school for the next three weeks. I'm leaving at 6:00 a.m. tomorrow and you are either coming with me or you can walk," Erin said as she walked away obviously frustrated.

Her point was made. I wasn't going to walk to school.

Looks like I better set my "opportunity clock" for 5:40 a.m. to get out the door with her at six o'clock.

What on earth was I going to do for two hours before school started? I wasn't sure if anyone would even be there.

CHAPTER 7
The 5:00 a.m. Club

When my iPhone alarm went off at 5:40 a.m., Erin was already fully showered, dressed, bags packed, and waiting for me.

"Joe, you got 20 minutes and I'm gone. I'm not waiting for you," Erin said in that tone of voice that all husbands know means it's time to get your act together.

I quickly jumped in the shower, got dressed in the same clothes I wore the day before (since they were conveniently left on the floor in the bathroom), grabbed my bag, and made it out the front door at 5:59 a.m., a record time for me in the last 15 years.

As I got in the car, she said, "Welcome to the 5:00 a.m. Club, Joe. Champions wake up while the clock says 5:00 a.m. Congratulations. Waking up early allows you to get a head start on your day and gives you more time to do things for yourself before the world starts pulling at you. You have to wake up early so you can make a personal and private investment into yourself before it becomes time to make a public investment into others."

I needed to start doing things for myself and never had time to do it. Maybe the 5:00 a.m. Club was the answer.

CHAPTER 8
The Mental Performance Daily Podcast
& The Success Hotline Podcast

Erin didn't talk much on the 15-minute drive to school. However, she did play two podcasts. The first was Mental Performance Daily with Brian Cain and the second was Success Hotline with Dr. Rob Gilbert.

Apparently, she had been listening to these two podcasts for years on her way to school. She would listen to the same three-minute recordings two times each on the way in.

When I asked her about it, she said it was like breakfast for her mind, food for her soul.

She said she had been listening to these podcasts every day for over 10 years. She shares what she learns each day with her students and has seen great results from sharing the messages. She said it was a critical part of her morning routine and a huge reason why she had closed the gap on achieving her goals both personally and professionally.

I had no idea that there was short, informational and inspiration podcasts that you could listen to each day for a little inspiration. That day, Brian Cain shared that the key to unlocking your potential was to be more intentional. He suggested that you needed to not count the days but make the days count.

Dr. Rob Gilbert had shared that there was nothing impossible, just time consuming and that all things were possible for those who were willing to put in the time and the training.

My only intention was to survive the day and take off one more number on my list of days left in the school year and the only thing I thought was possible was trying to survive this day.

However, I really enjoyed both The Mental Performance Daily Podcast and The Success Hotline Podcast and thought it might be a cool idea for me to start listening every day and then talking about it with Erin at night. We've been struggling to find things to talk about. Maybe this would be a good opener for us?

I could also use a little breakfast for my mind, and food for my soul if I was going to be getting up this early.

CHAPTER 9
The Ghost Town
of Bacon and Breakfast

Erin dropped me off at the front door to St. Joseph High School. Luckily, I didn't have to walk up "Heartbreak Hill," what I've come to call the quarter-mile walk from the parking lot up the hill to the school.

Much to my surprise, the front door was open and the school lights were on. There was nobody there, except I saw Mr. Mason's truck in the parking lot. He must have to be the first one there each day as the head custodian to open up the building.

As I made the walk to my classroom, I could smell the scent of bacon and the sweet aroma of freshly brewed coffee coming from the cafeteria. I hadn't been to the cafeteria in years, choosing always to eat the lunch I'd brought from home in the solitude of my classroom, taking advantage of what little quiet time I might get during the day.

This morning, the school felt like a ghost town. A school building that was normally bumping with kids and high-energy teachers, except for me was eerily quiet. The only signs of life were the reverberating hum of fluorescent light bulbs and the smell of fresh bacon and coffee.

CHAPTER 10
The Voice

As I set up shop in my classroom and waited for my computer to turn on, I found myself in unfamiliar territory. I sat there wondering what to do with all this extra time, then I heard a voice at my door.

"Mr. Big, what brings you here so early this mornin', sir?" a woman said as she leaned into my room.

"Oh, you know... just trying to get the year started off on the right foot, I guess. Trying to not count the days, but to make the days count," I responded.

"Don't count the days. Make the days count," she said with a smile shining from ear to ear. "Did you listen to The Mental Performance Daily Podcast this morning? Where did you get that one, Mr. Big?"

"As a matter of fact, I did," I said with a chuckle. "My wife listens every morning on her way to school. She played it twice actually. I had to ride in with her 'cause my car got water buggied yesterday."

"Oh. I see. The buggy gang got you," she said, laughing. "Well, look on the bright side: It could always have been worse. They could have buggied your car with you still in it."

We shared a laugh as I stood up from my desk and walked to the door.

"Joe Bigelow," I said, extending my hand. "Most people here call me Mr. Big."

"Sundra Torina," she responded. "Most people call me Sunny. I think it's because of my blonde hair, but I'd like to think it's because I bring a ray of sunlight with me wherever I go. You know, Mr. Big, the attitude you take is a decision you make.

"It's nice to officially meet you, Mr. Big. I work in the cafeterias here in the St Joseph School District, mostly here at the high school and will fill in at the elementary and middle schools when needed. Are you by any chance married to Mrs. Big at the elementary school?"

"Yes, that's Erin Bigelow, my wife," I answered with a smile.

"Oh my. I love me some Mrs. Big," Sunny said. "She sure does bring the juice to that school."

CHAPTER 11
Bring the Juice

"She does what?" I asked.

"She brings the juice, Mr. Big," Sunny said. "You know, she is enthusiastic and energized to teach every day. Her positive energy is infectious among her students and the other teachers. I always make it a point to say *Hello* to her when I'm there. As we like to say, 'If you're juiceful, you're useful, and if you're juiceless, you're useless.' She brings the juice every day. She is one of my favorites. Then again, all the people of the St. Joseph Schools are my favorites, but she is super special.

"Well, I need to get back to my breakfast and bacon. Nobody wants burnt bacon for breakfast, and breakfast is served at 7:00 a.m. each day here for our students. Why don't you come down and have some of Sunny's Bacon and Breakfast?"

I thanked her for stopping by and for her energy.

As Sunny left my classroom, I had to smile. Bring the juice. If you're juiceful, you're useful. I liked that. I just hadn't been bringing the juice like I did when I started teaching.

It was hard for me to get juiced up to do the same thing every day.

29

CHAPTER 12
No Bacon for Me...

I ended up not going to the cafeteria that morning for breakfast and bacon.

I decided to stay in the comfort zone of my classroom and do what I normally did: Wait for my students to show up, teach what I had been teaching for 20+ years, and then go home.

Luckily, that day I got a ride home from Mr. Mason, who drove right past our house. I had asked him about the possibility of catching a ride to school the next morning, but he got to school at 5:00 a.m. to unlock the building.

I thought leaving the house at 6:00 a.m. was early. I wanted no part of anything earlier than that!

As my head hit the pillow that night, Erin and I spoke about Sunny. Erin said that she learned about being juiceful from Sunny, and that being juiceful was part of her one percent better intention.

I didn't know what she meant by "her one percent better intention," but it was getting late, and I was exhausted from waking up so early. Knowing that this was how it was going to be for the next few weeks, I was ready to call it a night.

CHAPTER 13
Interested or Invested

The next morning was the same routine, except I got up a little earlier and put on some new clothes.

Just like yesterday, Erin and I listened to The Mental Performance Daily Podcast and The Success Hotline Podcast twice on the way to school. This time Brian Cain talked about how motion changes emotion, how movement changes moods, and how actions change attitudes. He said that we wake up our brains by sending a message from our feet that it's time to move and time to go.

As I entered the school and walked to my classroom, a sense of déjà vu engulfed me. There was no one in sight, but the familiar scent of bacon and breakfast permeated the halls.

After no more than five minutes in my classroom, Sunny popped her head into my room. This time, she was accompanied by a plate of bacon.

"Good morning, Mr. Big. I thought you might want some bacon to help you start bringing the juice this morning," Sunny said with a smile and laugh.

"Sunny, I'd love some," I replied.

As Sunny walked into the classroom with that plate of bacon, she sat down, and we chatted about

33

today's Mental Performance Daily Podcast and Success Hotline messages.

"You know, Mr. Big, what B. Cain talked about today on The MPD is truth. Motion does create emotion, movement does change moods, and action does change attitudes," Sunny said.

"It's why I get here early, not just to make the bacon and breakfast, but to walk the halls and start my day off with some movement. Just by walking I can feel the juice levels of my body climb from three to five to eight so that I can be at my best to serve my family—you know, the St. Joseph family of students and staff that are depending on me to provide them with a meal and a smile.

"But I haven't always had that perspective. I was more of the chicken than the pig. I was more interested than invested," she continued.

"I don't get it, Sunny. You lost me on the chicken and the pig piece." I was confused.

"Well, Mr. Big, think about it. For breakfast, every day we have eggs and we have bacon. Yes, we have some other items that rotate depending on the day of the week, but the two staples of each and every day are bacon and eggs," Sunny explained. "You can't have bacon and eggs without the chicken and the pig. Yet the chicken is interested in providing you breakfast, and the pig is fully committed, the pig is fully invested.

34

"With all due respect, sir, it's a lot like you and your wife as teachers. Mrs. Big is fully invested in her students and St. Joseph. I think you are just interested," Sunny said as her eyes pierced mine in a way I had not felt since I got done playing high school football for the legendary Coach John T. Allen.

"Sunny, you might be right. Erin is for sure more invested in her students and into the St. Joseph School District than I am," I said, feeling a little bit like I had been exposed or found out.

"Well, Mr. Big, the best time to plant the tree of investment and intention would have been 20+ years ago when you started, because it would be fully grown and able to provide fruit for others like your wife. But the second-best time to plant the tree is right now," Sunny stated as she stood up from my desk.

"I have to get back to the cafeteria to make sure I don't burn the bacon. Look, each morning while the bacon is cooking in the slow-simmer cooker we have that keeps all the juice in the bacon, I walk the halls to build up the juice inside of me for the day," Sunny said. "I've come to realize that a great school year is simply a by-product of great weeks, and great weeks are a by-product of stacking great days on top of great days. This mentality has allowed me to simply focus on being where my feet are and taking it day by day, very similar to taking it pitch by pitch as you might hear our JV softball coach, aka your wife, talk about."

"I have never thought of it like that, Sunny. Day by day to a great year. One day, or one pitch, at a time!" I exclaimed.

"It's like eating an elephant, Mr. Big. You have to do it bite by bite, not all at once. Inch by inch it's a cinch—and yard by yard it's hard. You know, Rome wasn't built in a day and it wasn't destroyed in a day ether. It's a process—a journey—and it all starts with your one percent better intention.

"Look here, Mr. Big. You have the number of days left in the school year hanging up in your classroom. Mrs. Big has the number **1** hanging up every day. Your intention is focusing on how many days we have left in the school year; her intention is how much can we accomplish on this very day? You are counting down the days till the end of the year, and she is making the days count. You are interested, she is invested. You are the chicken, and she is the pig in this metaphorical breakfast.

"By walking every day while I slow simmer the bacon, I am able to intentionally grow my fitness and my focus. I'd love for you to be my walking buddy in the morning this year, Mr. Big," Sunny said.

"Well, Sunny, I'm not much for walking, but what you have said today has really struck a tone with me. I want more out of my marriage, out of my teaching career, and out of life. I just feel stuck right now," I confessed, finally speaking the truth.

"Mr. Big, I got you. If you want more, you have to become more. And the only way to become more is to become more invested and more intentional. We talked today about being more invested. Tomorrow let's talk about being more intentional, but you are going to have to walk to continue our talk. I've been sitting long enough. Deal? You in?" Sunny asked with a smile, extending her hand for a shake of commitment.

"In," I said laughing. "Let's get juiced, make the days count, and be pigs."

For the first time in years, I was actually excited and looking forward to coming to school the next day. I wanted to drink more of Sunny's juice and become more.

CHAPTER 14
The One Percent Better Intention

The next morning was the same routine. Wake up, drive to school with Erin, listen to The Mental Performance Daily Podcast and The Success Hotline Podcast twice each on the way in. Walk into the building to the smell of bacon, except this time it was like Sunny knew I was there. She met me in my classroom as soon as I put my bags down.

"Good morning, Mr. Big! It's time to get juiced. Either we are going to dominate the day or the day will dominate us. Are you ready?" Sunny asked this with the excitement of a kid on Christmas day.

As we began walking the halls to the scent of bacon and breakfast, Sunny started asking me about math. "Mr. Big, there are 24 hours in a day and 60 minutes in each hour. How many minutes are there in a day?"

I quickly took out my phone and asked, "Hey, Siri. How many minutes in a day?"

"There are 1,440 minutes in a day," Siri chimed back.

Sunny and I both chuckled. Then she asked, "What's one percent of 1,440?"

This is where I was stumped. I wasn't sure how to do the math. After all, I wasn't a math teacher.

"No idea," I replied.

"One percent of a day is 14 minutes and 24 seconds," she said emphatically. "Everyone wants to get one percent better, but they fail to intentionally invest one percent of their day into getting better because they don't even know that it's a strategy for success.

"Mr. Big, I walk the halls every morning for 14 minutes and 24 seconds, and that's my one percent better intention. I've been doing it for years since I learned the strategy from Mr. Guzzo, our activities director. By walking for 14:24 every morning—whether I feel like it or not—I am able to create a domino effect of positivity in my life that creates the energy I need to serve others for that full day.

"Most people go through life on a treadmill. They wake up and do the same thing every day. They don't live with any intention; they merely exist by going through the motions. They drive to school the same way, eat the same thing, talk to the same people, doing pretty much the same thing every day, and it's unintentional. The first step to growth, change, development, and becoming more so you can do, be, and have more, is to become more intentional.

"The best place to start is to intentionally invest one percent of your day into getting one percent better yourself and into becoming a better version of you today than you were yesterday. Then wake up tomorrow and do the same thing. Rinse and repeat. It's actually quite simple, Mr. Big."

She was making a lot of sense. I was on the treadmill of life. I had no intentions other than taking down the number of days on my wall till the next summer. Sunny was right; the place for me to start to become more was to be more intentional by creating my one percent better intention.

CHAPTER 15
Better or Bitter

"You know, Mr. Big, Mr. Weston and other administrators have to put teachers who underperform on professional development plans," Sunny stated. "I think that everyone should ALWAYS have their own professional development plan. If you don't have a plan, how are you getting better? The problem is when you stop getting better, you start getting bitter, and ain't nobody like being around people who are bitter all the time."

"Sunny, I feel like you know me well. I'm not intentional and have been more bitter than I'd like to admit," I said. "Mr. Weston put me on a professional development plan at school and my wife put me on a personal development plan at home. In all actuality, I need to PUT MYSELF on a personal and professional development plan, not because they want me to be on one, but because I want to be on one so I can be more intentional."

"EXACTLY!" Sunny said. "And the simplest form of a personal or professional development plan is to do have a one percent better intention, to do something intentional for one percent—or 14:24— of your day.

"Mr. Big, our walk time is coming to a close today. I have to get back to my bacon and breakfast. Here's what I want you to do: I want you to create a one percent better intention where seven minutes and twelve seconds are intentionally invested into your personal development, and seven minutes and twelve seconds are intentionally invested into your professional development.

"This will create your one percent better intention and get you started so you can build momentum towards your personal and professional development. This one percent better intention very well could save your marriage and save your job. Tomorrow, I want you to bring me a written plan of what your one percent better intention will be. Deal?" Sunny said as she extended her hand in my direction.

"Deal!" I exclaimed.

CHAPTER 16
Change Is Inevitable;
Growth Is Optional

I went back into my classroom and remembered what Brian Cain had said on The Mental Performance Daily Podcast that morning: *Change is inevitable; growth is optional.*

My fitness had changed.

My students had changed.

My marriage had changed.

My motivation for teaching had changed.

Meeting Sunny and learning from her as well as my new morning podcast routine had really opened up my eyes. Change is inevitable. We live in an ever-changing world, but growth is optional.

You will automatically change as you get older and as your life ticks away, but growth only happens by your intention.

I finally felt like I had a plan to grow intentionally, and that plan was my one percent better intention. It was time for me to write out what I was going to do each day to more intentionally grow into the best version of myself. I wanted—no, I NEEDED—to become more juiceful, to stop counting the days and start making the days count, so I could stop getting dominated by the day and start dominating the day.

My first step was to take down the days left in the school year, put up the number **1**, and to talk about the importance of the day. I could use that as an opportunity to share with my students how yesterday was history, tomorrow is a mystery, and that today is a gift. That's why we call it the present.

After I took down the numbers, I sat and mapped out my one percent better intention plan for my personal and professional development.

CHAPTER 17
Mr. Big's One Percent Better Intention

Waking up in the 5:00 a.m. Club was getting much easier. I enjoyed my early morning time with my wife. I enjoyed our ride to school listening to the two podcasts together.

I was still looking forward to getting my car back, but at the same time, I was enjoying the new routine.

When I got to my classroom, it wasn't more than a minute before I heard Sunny.

"Mr. Big, do you have your one percent better intention to show me?" she asked with inquisitiveness.

"As a matter of fact, I do. It's right here," I said as I pulled out my one percent better intention.

PERSONAL DEVELOPMENT
- 3:00 – Mental Performance Daily Podcast

- 3:00 – Success Hotline Podcast

- 1:12 – Hold a plank for core strength

PROFESSIONAL DEVELOPMENT

- 3:00 – Study the names and faces of all St. Joseph High School employees.

- 4:12 – Write down the class learning objectives on the board for the day and write out the main message from Mental Performance Daily and Success Hotline that day so I can share this with my students.

"Mr. Big... this is tremendous. You now have a legitimate personal and professional development plan that YOU OWN because you created it," Sunny said. "People don't usually get down on what they are in on, and you were super in on creating this plan because you chose intentions that are very meaningful to you personally and professionally."

"You know, Sunny, I felt stuck when my wife and Mr. Weston put me on the personal and professional development plans. I just wasn't motivated because I was being told what to do rather than taking personal ownership. I was acting like a victim instead of a victor. You led me to the one percent better intention, and I truly believe that if I execute this plan, I will take steps, although seemingly small, towards the person I want to become," I declared.

"Mr. Big, it's the start that stops most people. An object, in this case you, in motion stays in motion. It's breaking inertia that is the hardest part. Did you know that a space shuttle uses about 80% of its fuel in the first hour of its journey? Once you get momentum on your side, success comes your way. You create a rhythm and routine and start operating your habits and routines more intentionally instead of blindly going through the motions. I like to call it *growing* through the motions vs. *going* through the motions," Sunny asserted.

"The best place to start is always with your one percent better intention. Your one percent better intention is flexible and flowing. It can adapt over time, but it must ALWAYS be written down and it must always be in action, preferably as a part of your a.m. or p.m. routine because that's where you have most of the control of your day."

"I also see you now have the number 1 up in your classroom and this is not the last day of the year. Are you being more intentional about not counting the days but making the days count?" Sunny asked.

"You don't miss a thing, do you, Sunny?" I said with a smile. "Yes, it's all about today. I have realized from our talks that Today + Today + Today = the School Year, and I want this to be the best year of my career. I now realize that will only happen if I go day by day with a new level of juice and a new level of intentionality."

49

"Mr. Big, you got it. Now the question is are you going to be legendary or temporary?" Sunny asked.

CHAPTER 18
Legendary or Temporary

"It's very common for people to get energized and excited when they learn something new, but it's consistency that unlocks all of the doors to optimal performance," Sunny continued. "We want to keep your focused on getting one percent better by working your intentional plan, a plan so simple and executable that you can do it consistently day to day and become legendary. When you make plans that are too broad or too hard so that you only do it for a short period of time, we call that temporary. The key is to be legendary with the execution of your one percent better intention, not temporary."

"Legendary or temporary. That makes sense. But how do you do that exactly?" I asked.

"Well, I'm glad you asked," Sunny replied. "Brian Cain shared a system and process for this today on Mental Performance Daily. Let's go over it."

CHAPTER 19
A + S + GOYA = R

"Today's Mental Performance Daily Podcast was about exactly how to go from temporary to legendary. B. Cain talked about A + S + GOYA = R," Sunny explained.

I was glad she was going over this because on the ride in this morning I didn't quite pick up what Brian Cain was putting down. He was super excited and talked really fast.

"B. Cain is using an acronym that means *Ability + Strategy + Get Off Your Anatomy and do the work = Results*," Sunny recited aloud as she wrote it on the white board in my classroom. "Mr. Big, ability is not something you are lacking to be the optimal version of yourself. You are simply *blocking* it. How we unblock our ability is by giving you the right strategy. In this case, that strategy is simply your one percent better intention plan. You then have to get off your anatomy and do your one percent better intention each day. When you do that, you will see better results."

I nodded my head in agreement. This was all making perfect sense to me. I was blocking my ability by not having a strategy for development. And since I did not have a strategy, I was not motivated to get off my anatomy, and thus my results were not what I was looking for.

"Once you accept that you have all the ability inside of you and you get a strategy, one of the best things you can do is find an accountability partner who you will share your one percent better intention plan with. You need someone in your corner who will work with you to create more clarity and provide more accountability and support," Sunny explained.

"An accountability partner is something that learned about when I went through Brian, I call him B. Cain's Mental Performance Mastery Coaching Certification Course. It was great, something that I think every teacher should do for professional development."

"I have been your accountability partner this week and will be for this month, but at the end of the month I want you to share your knowledge and share the juice by being an accountability partner with another person in the building. This way, you can grow your social network and personal development team and together we can achieve more. You know, the bigger your goals, the bigger a team you are going to need.

"Remember this, Mr. Big," Sunny said as she took a step closer to me...

CHAPTER 20
In You Before In What You Do

"Your one percent intention must be in you before it shows up in what you do," Sunny said. "You must embody that which you want to share with others. You CANNOT give to others that which you do not first personally possess. If you want other people to be juiced, you must first be juiced yourself. If you want others to be intentional, you must first be intentional yourself.

"If you want people to grow on a personal or professional development plan, that plan must be inside of them, or in this case inside of YOU," Sunny said, putting a finger on my chest, "before it comes out in what you do." She pointed to all of the empty chairs in my classroom.

That made so much sense to me. I remember Erin telling me that the content we teach is caught more than taught. That our students will "catch" our curriculum before it's taught to them. Two teachers can say exactly the same thing, but the way in which the message is delivered or the presentation style that's utilized is going to be caught first.

"Sunny, my one percent better intention is mine. I created it. I own it. I want to do it. I just need your help this month to keep me on course so that I can go from temporary to legendary and be more juiceful and useful to those I teach and to those I love." I fought back tears of emotion as I felt like the new energized and juiced me that had been blocked and lying dormant for years was finally coming out.

"Mr. Big, I got you. Just commit to paying it forward. We have this month to get your mind right and then you are going to need to share what you have learned with someone else. Together we can impact as many people in the St. Joseph School District as possible." Sunny once again extended her hand for me to shake on it.

"A deal's a deal, Sunny. Thank you," I responded as I shook her hand.

"Oh, by the way, you are standing in a high five zone," I said, pointing to a poster on my classroom wall that I had hung up the day before. It had a picture of a hand that said *The High Five Zone* across it in bold text.

"High fives are free, Sunny, and they are a great way to help spread the juice." I raised my hand to give her five.

"High fives *are* free!" Sunny said as she slapped me five. We both smiled and laughed as she pointed to me and said, "Remember, it's gotta be in you before it's in what you do! I love that high five zone Mr. Big, I am stealing that."

Then she walked back to the cafeteria to make sure that she didn't burn her bacon and breakfast.

CHAPTER 21
The 3 Step Success Cycle & The 4 Step Goal Formula

Waking up earlier was getting easier—to the point where I started looking forward to those first few moments before the rest of the world woke from its slumber—a time I'd intentionally avoided for over a decade. I noticed that since setting my one percent better intention, I had more energy and more enthusiasm, and was more positive at school and at home.

My wife had even noticed and said that she was proud of me for creating a one percent better intention and actually following through and executing on it, granted it had been for less than a week.

The next day I showed up at school bright and early, but this time when I walked in, Sunny was already in my classroom, bacon in hand.

"Mr. Big, I wanted to get here early today to share with you what I call *The 3 Step Success Cycle* and *The 4 Step Goal Formula.* Knowing these processes is going to be critical to your sustained success and to strengthening your process around the execution of your one percent better intention. First let me share with you The 3 Step Success Cycle."

THE 3 STEP SUCCESS CYCLE

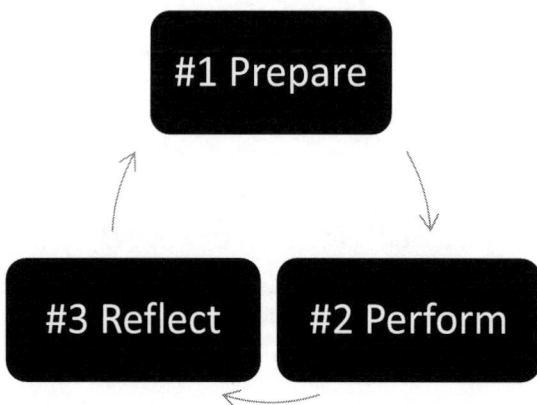

#1 Prepare

#3 Reflect   **#2 Perform**

"When you create a one percent better intention, you want to be sure that you then follow The 3 Step Success Cycle. The 3 Step Success Cycle is a process that is applied to all types of performance, teaching, marriage, athletics, business—and yes, your one percent better intention," Sunny said.

"First, you have to prepare for your performance. Then, you perform. Finally, you have to reflect on your performance to maximize your learning from that performance or that day. The biggest mistake I see in people who set the one percent better intention is that they prepare by writing down what they will do, then they do their one percent better intention for a short period of time but fail to reflect on it. Reflection is where the golden nuggets of wisdom and development are mined. You have to reflect so you can learn. Otherwise, you slip back into going through the motions instead of *growing* through the motions," Sunny explained.

All my life I had focused on preparing and then performing. In my teaching career, I had prepared for so many years that I felt like I didn't really need to anymore. I just taught the same material each year so my preparation process was minimal.

I didn't EVER spend time in reflection. I think it's because I would be scared of what I saw.

I loved what Sunny was saying about reflection being where the golden nuggets of wisdom and development were mined.

"Sunny, I can see where The 3 Step Success Cycle comes into play. I must reflect on my one percent better intention each day and each week, but what's The 4 Step Goal Formula?"

"Mr. Big, I am glad you asked. The 3 Step Success Cycle and The 4 Step Goal Formula go hand in hand," Sunny replied. "The 4 Step Goal Formula is as follows..."

THE 4 STEP GOAL FORMULA

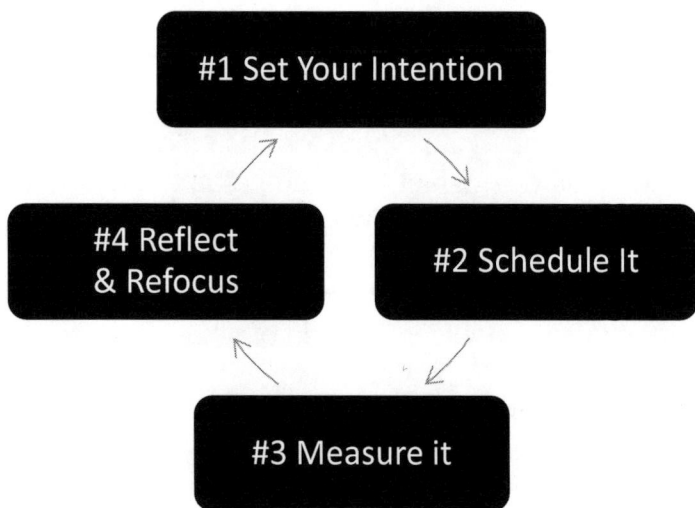

#1 Set Your Intention

#4 Reflect & Refocus

#2 Schedule It

#3 Measure it

"With The 4 Step Goal Formula you first set your intention, as you did when you wrote your 14:24, one percent better intention. The reason why writing it down is so important is that when you write down your intention, you take it from the clouds and you put it in the dirt. Where do things grow, Mr. Big? In the clouds or the dirt?" Sunny asked.

"In the dirt," I replied.

"EXACTLY!" Sunny exclaimed. "If you leave your intention in your head, which most people do, you are leaving it in the clouds. And stuff doesn't grow in the clouds. It grows in dirt. It's moving from just talking the talk to actually walking the walk. You have to write your intention down on paper. When you do that, you are taking your one percent better intention from the clouds (your head) to the dirt (paper) so that it can grow—or in this case, so that you can share it with others and... SCHEDULE IT.

"Once you SET your one percent better intention, you then need to SCHEDULE it. I always encourage folks to schedule it as part of their a.m. or p.m. routine because that is where we have the most control in our lives. Once we schedule it, we need to do step three of MEASURE IT because measurement is motivation and data doesn't lie. It tells the truth," Sunny said. "I use a free app on my phone called Habit Share to help me measure my progress. I used to just use a daily success checklist with paper and pencil but what I love about habit share is that I can add you as a friend so you can see what I am doing for added support and accountability as my accountability partner."

"You can have the best plan in the world, but if you don't schedule it, you are less likely to execute it. Similarly, if you do schedule it but don't measure it, you don't know if you are being consistent in executing your one percent better intention. Consistent execution of a simple personal and professional growth plan is exactly how we close the gap from where we are to where we want to be. And make no mistake, Mr. Big. We all have gaps.

"We have gaps in our professional and personal lives. We have gaps in our education and our health and wellness. We have gaps in our leadership and our relationships. And the secret is to know that you NEVER will close the gaps completely. You will never be perfect, but perfection is NOT the goal. The goal is progress and closing the gaps in our lives is what setting our one percent better intention helps us to do.

"The problem is that most people are so busy living in an external world of Instagram, Facebook, Twitter, TikTok and TV that they never go into their internal world and reflect on who they really are, who they really want to be, and what they really want to do with their life. It's because we live in the external world and never go internal that most people seek happiness instead of fulfillment.

"Happiness comes and goes like the wind. Fulfillment is what we are really after. Being fulfilled comes from living in alignment with who you want to be, and what you want to do.

"Look, I gotta to get back to my bacon. But tomorrow I will talk with you about the MVP Process. If you intentionally create your one percent better intention along with an MVP process and then you align those two strategies, I can pretty much guarantee your growth and progress towards the best and most optimal Mr. Big we have ever seen. But you got to be invested; you can't just be interested. We ain't makin' any bacon with chickens," Sunny said, laughing as she walked towards me.

"Tomorrow we go over the MVP Process and how you can be the MVP of your own life, Mr. Big. Deal?" Sunny said as she extended her hand in my direction.

"Deal!" I said as I reached out my hand and shook on it. "See you in the morning. I need to start reflecting and measuring my one percent better intention."

CHAPTER 22
The Daily Success Checklist

When Sunny left my room that day, I went back to my desk and grabbed my phone. Except this time, instead of looking at ESPN.com, I opened up the app store and got the *Habit Share* app and started creating a daily success checklist for myself and my one percent better intention.

The dates for the week were across the top and then what I was going to do for my one percent better intention was on the left. I had a check box under each date so that I could check off the days I executed my one percent better intention and easily reflect on my performance to measure progress at the end of the week. I was going to do my personal one percent better intention seven days per week and my professional one percent better intention five days a week, Monday through Friday.

Date:	M	T	W	TH	F	S	SU
Personal							
Mental Performance Daily							
Success Hotline							
Plank Hold							
Professional							
Study St. Joseph Staff							
Write Out Objectives							
Write Out MPD/SH							

As I measured my progress, I could really see how The 3 Step Success Cycle and The 4 Step Goal Formula played a crucial role in my personal and professional development.

Each day that I checked off the box in executing my one percent better intention was like lifting weights. I was becoming stronger from the inside out by doing a little a lot—and not a lot a little. I had been paralyzed for so long by looking at the entire elephant, and now I was making progress towards eating the elephant by going one bite at a time.

CHAPTER 23
ONE, The Magic Number

The next day when I walked into the school, something was different. There was still the same smell of bacon and breakfast permeating from the café. The building was still a ghost town; Mr. Mason, Sunny and I were probably the only people on campus. But today there was music playing:

> *ONE, it's the magic number.*
> *ONE, it's all you need.*
> *ONE, it's the magic number.*
> *ONE, it's the growth seed.*

The voice on the school PA system sounded familiar. I just couldn't put my thumb on who it belonged to.

When I finally got to my classroom, Sunny was already in there. I immediately saw balloons with **ONE** printed on them tied to the chairs in the room. Glancing up at the white board, I noticed **ONE** was written in big, bold strokes.

"Is it someone's first birthday today, Sunny?" I asked with a chuckle.

"No, it's opening day of the school year. Come to think of it, every day is opening day," she said with a smile. "Mr. Big, do you remember when you were first hired here in St. Joseph some 20+ years ago? How excited you were for the first day of school?

Sure, you were a little nervous, but nervousness is really just excitement without the breath."

"Oh yeah, I remember," I answered. "It was a day I will never forget."

"Well, why don't you live every day like it's opening day? Or why don't you teach today like you are on a one-day contract and your performance determines if you get to come back or not? Wouldn't you bring the juice if it were opening day? Wouldn't you prepare, perform, and then reflect if you knew you had a one-day contract to teach here at St. Joseph?"

"Yeah, I would for sure be more intentional, more prepared, and bring the juice. I'd be a lot more uncomfortable too. That's for sure!" I exclaimed.

"And that's where the magic happens, when we get out of our comfort zone and enter the growth zone! We were going to talk about the MVP Process today, but that can wait till tomorrow. For today, let's focus on this number right here," Sunny said pointing to the **ONE** she had drawn on the board. "ONE, it's the magic number," she sang, laughing.

"That was you!!!" I exclaimed, laughing out loud. "That was you on the school PA today."

"Oh yeah. I think it's a mix of Cardi B and Madonna, but I'll let you make your own conclusion on that one, Mr. Big." Sunny laughed harder than I had ever seen her laugh.

"Let's get right into it. What do you already know about the number One, Mr. Big?" Sunny asked.

I stood up, walked to the board and began to write.

One day at a time.
One pitch at a time.
One student at a time.
One step at a time. Be where your feet are.
ONE = Only Need Everyone.
One percent better intention.
1%

Inside of the slash in the one percent I wrote "14:24."

1%

I thought this was a cool visual way to represent the one percent. Sunny agreed as she tossed knuckles my way followed by a high five.

"I love it! WOW, Mr. Big! That's fabulous. Let me share one more thing about the magic number one with you.

"Here, take this white band." Sunny handed me a white silicone band with the words *ONE PERCENT BETTER* on it.

"On this band, you have the words *ONE PERCENT BETTER*. You also have a lot of white space. In one of these white spaces, I want you to write the word *INTENTION* as a reminder for you to be more intentional about how you live your life and to execute your one percent better intention.

Sunny then handed me a black Sharpie pen. I wrote the word *INTENTION*.

"Mr. Big, the reason why I didn't have the word *INTENTION* embossed on the band is because you have to revisit your ONE PERCENT BETTER INTENTION frequently or it will fade away. You are going to have to write the word *INTENTION* on your band every few days, or that will disappear, and so will your commitment to your personal and professional development.

"You know, Mr. Big, the best way to learn something is to teach it." Sunny smiled as she handed me a big bag of the bands and a box of Northeast airline peanuts they hand out during flights.

"I want you to share this exercise with your students today because ONE is the magic number. You know what the bands are for. The peanuts... those are to be eaten ONE peanut at a time to reinforce the importance of presence and the commitment to doing things one at a time.

"My sister works for Northeast and she says that most people will just dump the whole bag in their mouths at once. I want you to eat one peanut at a time and have your students do the same. You will laugh at how challenging it can be to simply be where your feet are and go one peanut at a time. Can you do that today with your classes?" Sunny asked, again extending her hand in my direction.

"Deal!" I said. "Give each student one band and one bag of peanuts with strict instructions to eat only one at a time and to write the word intention and on the band. Roger that, Sunny."

CHAPTER 24
The Best Day of My Career

That day I will never forget.

It was the greatest day of my professional career.

When my students walked in, they saw the balloons, but most importantly, they saw me standing in the high five zone welcoming them all into the room with juice, a smile and a high five connection.

I explained why the **ONE** was on the board and talked about how the greatest gift we can give is our presence. Then I shared with my students how one number and meeting one person—Sunny— had changed my life in the last week.

I shared with them that their best mindset to graduate from high school, to get into the college of their choice, and to have the life of their dreams was to simply eat the elephant one bite at a time and to be totally invested like the pig.

It was a day where I totally connected with my students. I had struggled for years to connect with them. I had focused too much on content and not enough on human connection. I had forgotten that I was here to teach people, not content.

That day, we didn't crack a textbook. We cracked the barrier between us and built a connection that I hadn't felt since my first days of teaching.

Mr. Weston had told me in our meeting where he put me on a professional development plan that I needed to build better connection with my students. He said students won't care what I know until they know that I care.

I agreed with him. I just struggled to find a way to connect and show them that I cared.

That day changed my life.

As I sat there with my students and listened to each of them share their ONE PERCENT BETTER INTENTION to become the best versions of themselves, while we all ate peanuts one at a time, I felt connection growing between us all that I had never felt in my classroom before.

I didn't want the classes to end. Normally I couldn't wait to get out of school. That day I didn't want the bell to ring.

I was in my element. I was educating, empowering, and energizing others to become their best.

CHAPTER 25
Emotional Breakthrough

The next day I was in my room promptly at 6:20 a.m. Sunny walked in with her plate of bacon, something that had become a customary part of our morning routine.

"Well, how did it go with the ONE PERCENT BETTER bands and the peanuts with your students yesterday, Mr. Big?" Sunny asked.

"Sunny...." I started before swallowing a lump in my throat.

Emotion was flooding through my veins like a tidal wave. Yesterday was the most magical day of my teaching career, and the woman I had to thank for it was sitting five feet from me asking me about it.

I started to cry. I was overcome with joy and emotion that I had not felt in years.

"I'm sorry, Sunny," I said.

"Sorry for what, Mr. Big?" Sunny asked, moving closer to me as she put her arms on my shoulders. "Those are tears of joy. That's the juice coming out of you, my brother. You are having an emotional breakthrough; it's your spirit being released because you are fulfilled and finally aligning how you behave with who you want to be and what you want to do. Tell me about yesterday."

I wiped away tears from my eyes and cleared the lump of juice from my throat. "Sunny, yesterday I felt the strongest connection to my students that I have ever felt in 20+ years of teaching.

"We didn't talk about content—heck, we didn't even open a textbook! We built connection. Students shared their one percent better intentions. Some students laughed, some cried, and some just didn't get it," I said with a laugh.

"Just didn't get it YET..." Sunny said. "They will catch it if you keep bringing it."

"You're right, Sunny," I replied. "Yesterday was the first day that I felt like what I had to give was worth catching. I have you to thank for that."

"Mr. Big, please thank yourself. You are the one who did all the work. I'm just happy to have someone to share my bacon with in the morning," Sunny said with a laugh. "This is a big step towards being the person St. Joseph needs you to be, Mr. Big. For years you have given St. Joseph your B-game. You may have given the best of what you had, but what you had wasn't your best.

"No more, sir! It's time that St. Joseph gets to experience the real Mr. Big, the dude that Mrs. Big fell in love with in college and the dude that was voted Teacher of the Year in all of St. Joseph School District in just his first year. I was at that commencement speech you gave; that was

juiceful. Look, I still have the ACE card you passed
out that day to the graduating class."

CHAPTER 26
The Four ACE Cards

Sunny pulled out a business-sized card with an ACE of spades on one side and the following four statements on the other side:

Acting Changes Energy
Awareness Creates Engagement
Attitude Creates Excellence
Action Changes Everything

I was blown away. I had given out that ACE card at graduation nearly 20 years ago when I had won Teacher of the Year in my first year of teaching. The graduating senior class had selected me to give the commencement address.

On that day, I gave each graduating senior an ACE card and talked about "The Four ACEs of Life."

I talked about how Acting Changes Energy. That you have to learn to let your actions change your feelings instead of letting your feelings dictate your actions. I talked about how all great performers and achievers acted as if they were successful before they became successful.

And I talked about the importance of awareness and how Awareness Creates Engagement, and that awareness was the precursor to all change and growth, because with awareness comes focus and where your focus goes energy flows and that your focus determines your future.. The more aware you are of who you are, who you want to be, and what you want to do, the more engagement and focus you can direct in those areas to improve your chances at success.

In addition, I spoke about how your Attitude Creates Excellence and that excellence is doing your best to how a commitment to excellence is actually a commitment to fulfillment. Most people think that winning is excellence, but it's not. Winning and excellence are very different: Winning is an outcome. Excellence is a lifestyle knowing that there is no finish line and that you must keep charging ahead in face of both success and failure to be better today than yesterday and better tomorrow than today.

Finally, I talked about how Action Changes Everything. How if you wanted to go somewhere or do something in life, it was dependent on a lot of factors, but the most important factor was and always would be YOU and what you DO on a daily basis. The ACTIONS that you take determine the strides that you make.

I had not talked about the Four ACE cards in years and was certainly not living them intentionally... well, until I started to meet with Sunny.

"Sunny, that's amazing. You were at my commencement address 20 years ago and we are just finally meeting now? How is that possible?"

"Mr. Big, a lot of people think that things happen for a reason—I don't. I don't believe that hope and fate are effective strategies for success. I believe you share your future; you speak it, you make it real and tangible by talking about it, visualizing it and then you go to work relentlessly on creating it," Sunny answered. "And, of course, you must adapt and adjust as life happens because you can't prepare for everything. We must be willing to stay flexible in our abilities to adapt and adjust.

"I believe that there is a reason why things happen more than things happen for a reason. I believe the power is within us and our choices more than anything else. I like to take total responsibility for my life. I was at your commencement that day because my daughter was a senior the year you were a first-year teacher.

"We have not met because over the last 20+ years I have been at the elementary school in their cafeteria and just got hired here last year. I didn't meet you last year because you never left your classroom and were never here early enough for us to cross paths on my morning bacon walk," Sunny explained.

"I sure am glad we got to meet, though, Mr. Big. Unfortunately, we had a cafeteria worker at the elementary school, Mrs. Edie, move out of the district this week to take a full-time job at a school in Aruba. Sure, can't fault her for that, but now we are a little thin at the elementary school, so I will be going back down there at the end of this week.

"I did want to make sure that we covered how to be the MVP of your own life before I go. Can you get here a little earlier tomorrow so we have more time? Can you get here at 6:00 a.m. sharp?" Sunny asked as she extended her hand toward me.

"A deal's a deal. I'll be here at 6:00 a.m.," I replied.

CHAPTER 27
The MVP Process

That night I told Erin that I had to be at school by 6:00 a.m. the next morning. She didn't ask why; she just smiled and said she was proud of me. When I told her I was meeting with Sunny, she smiled, laughed, and said, "I love that woman."

The next day I was in my classroom at 6:00 a.m. when in walked Sunny with—you guessed it—her plate of bacon.

"Mr. Big, are you ready to become the MVP of your own life?"

"Sunny, I am ready for whatever you want to give me. I'd probably even have walked to school this morning if Erin didn't want to get up so early," I replied.

"Mrs. Big is an early riser, I'm sure," Sunny said with a smile.

"She is a member of the 5:00 a.m. Club, no doubt about it." We both laughed.

"Mr. Big, since this is our last formal morning meeting before I head back down to the elementary school, I wanted to first commend you on your growth. In just a little more than a week I have seen tremendous growth in you due to your new daily focus of setting a one percent better intention. But for you to continue to thrive and not fall back into a routine where you are just trying to survive, like you have been doing for the last few years, we need to strengthen your one percent better intention by creating an MVP Process.

"The MVP Process is an acronym for Mission, Vision, and Principles. All great schools have a staff who are on a collective mission, have a shared vision, and behave based on a set of intentionally determined core principles," Sunny continued.

"Every successful school, business, athletic team, or individual I have ever read about or worked with has had an intentionally designed MVP Process, whether they called it that or not. We have an MVP Process here in the St. Joseph School District. Do you know what it is?"

"Sunny, I know that we have a mission, vision, and principles because I have seen the poster on the wall, but I couldn't tell you what they are," I admitted.

"Neither could most people in the school district," Sunny said. "The problem with that is if you pay lip service to a mission statement but don't have people actually on a mission, then you don't really have a mission statement. All you have is a poster on a wall. Sadly, that's how it is in most schools, teams and organizations in the world.

"The Mission, Vision, and Core Principles have to be in you before they will ever show up in what you do. It's why one of my goals, if we had more time together, would be to work with you on creating you own personal MVP Process. I think that if we go over the MVP Process for St. Joseph Schools, you will easily be able to duplicate that process for yourself.

"Remember, to be consistent at anything, we must be able to describe what we do as a process. Your one percent better intention is a process that you set, schedule, and measure to make sure that you are growing personally and professionally. Because if you ain't growing, you are dying—and we got a heck of a lot of living to do, Mr. Big, even in my seventies."

CHAPTER 28
The Mission

"A lot of people, schools, and organizations use the terms 'mission' and 'vision' interchangeably. That happens because they fail to define or create a simple picture to illustrate how they are different. Let me simplify for you, Mr. Big," Sunny said.

"Think about mission as your tombstone: What you want people to say about you when you are gone. A good mission has NO FINISH LINE.

"The mission of St. Joseph Schools is to *Inspire lifelong learners and create tomorrow's leaders.* That's a journey and a process that has no finish line. We will be doing that as long as the St. Joseph Schools exist.

"My personal mission, Mr. Big, what I want on my tombstone is that I *Educated, empowered and energized others to be their best.*

"Mr. Big, I want you to write out your personal mission before your head hits the pillow tonight. Make sure that your one percent better intention aligns with your personal mission so that you can be sure that you are making progress towards becoming the best version of yourself each and every day."

CHAPTER 29
The Vision

"Vision is different than mission in that it's your resume, not your tombstone. You want your vision to be very tangible, measurable, and able to be answered with a simple *Yes* or *No,*" Sunny explained.

"The vision of the St. Joseph Schools is laid out like a staircase. It's a process that builds upon the step that comes before it. The vision is:

100% Graduation Rate
Top 5% Performance Nationally

90%+ Community, Parent, and Student
Engagement and Satisfaction
Continued Enrollment Growth

100% Literacy Rate
Financial Stability
Inspire a Lifelong Learner Today

"We put *Inspire a Lifelong Learner Today* as the bottom step because that's what we want to do on a daily basis, and we want that to be our primary focus in interacting with students."

Sunny stated, "When you had the big breakthrough with your students the other day, it was largely related to your ability to inspire a lifelong learner on that day. You made a connection, and always remember that connection comes before content in teaching, leadership and mentorship.

"My personal vision is to complete a marathon in my seventies, to open up my own lemon-with-vanilla frosted cupcake business this year called 'Sunny's Delights,' visit my friend in Aruba, volunteer for the French Bulldogs for Fighters Foundation once a month and execute my one percent better intention each day.

"You can see, Mr. Big," Sunny continued, "that all the steps on my vision can easily be answered with a *Yes* or *No* at the end of the day.

"Now it's your turn," she said, pointing a finger toward my chest. "I want you to write out your personal vision before your head hits the pillow tonight. You don't have to get it done, but you do have to get it started. Remember, it's the start that stops most people. Once you write out your vision, please check to make sure it aligns with your mission as well as with your one percent better intention, so that you can be sure you are making progress towards becoming the best version of yourself each and every day."

CHAPTER 30
The Core Principles

"The core principles that you set as a school, team, organization, or as an individual are very similar to having a set of core values. I call them 'core principles' because getting people to remember MVP Process is easier than MVV," Sunny explained with a laugh.

"The reason why core principles are important is so that you can start to move from living out of *preference* into living out of *principle*. Most people live their life out of preference, doing what feels good or makes them happy in the moment. Elite, world-class performers realize the difference between short-term happiness and long-term fulfillment. They realize that to be fulfilled you must start by intentionally setting your core principles, and then aligning your core principles, mission, and vision with your one percent better intentional growth plan and ultimately your day-to-day behavior.

"Once you set core principles, you then have to define what those principles mean so that operationally everyone can have a chance to be on the same page with their definitions.

"Here in the St. Joseph Schools, our core principles are simply remembered by the acronym DEPICT:

Diversity

Acceptance of all, and celebration of our differences.

Excellence

Work to be the best version of yourself.

PRIDE

Personal Responsibility In Daily Effort.

Integrity

Do what's right at all times.

Compassion

Unconditionally give of yourself to others.

Teamwork

We before me.

"My personal core values are the acronym APPLE:

Accountability

Doing what's right and DWYSWYD

Present

Be where your feet are

Process

Have a plan and stick to it

Love

Unconditionally give of yourself

Energy

Bring the juice

"If you look at any of my social media Mr. Big, you will see I often post three green apples. The three represents my mission to Educate, Empower and Energize, the green means GO and APPLE means... well... APPLE. My principles."

"Mr. Big, just like you are going to write out your mission and vision, I also want you to write out your personal core principles before your head hits the pillow tonight. Start with one principle and a definition and then work from there. You don't have to get it right; you just have to get it started. Remember, it's the start that stops most people.

Once you write out your core principles, please then check to make sure they align with your mission, vision, and your one percent better intention so that you can be sure you are making progress towards becoming the best version of yourself each and every day.

CHAPTER 31
The Next Steps

"Sunny... This is amazing. You are amazing!" I said with humility, as I finished taking down my notes from her discussion of the MVP Process.

"You know in 20+ years at St. Joseph, I have never had it broken down to me that simply. I now finally understand the difference between mission, vision, and principles. I get the importance of having an MVP process so that the teachers and staff of The St. Joseph School District can all be on the same page and have a collective mission, shared vision, and a set of core principles to assure student success," I said.

"I also now understand that the MVP Process must be in you before it's in what you do. I've never heard it put that way. And I now realize that if I am going to be able to live out the MVP Process at St. Joseph, I must have an MVP process that I am living in my own life. I can never give or become that which I don't have, and Sunny, I will never go through another day of my life without having a personal mission, a personal vision, a set of core principles and a one percent better intention that I execute for 14:24 of each day.

"I can't thank you enough for your time over the last two weeks and for making the investment in me that you have. How can I ever repay you?"

"Mr. Big, it's been my pleasure, sir," Sunny stated with a smile. "The way for you to repay me is to pay it forward and share what you have learned with others. Share what you have learned here with your students, with Mrs. Big, and with other teachers and staff in the building that you think may be stuck in a rut or who have lost their intention."

"Sunny, I will do that. One last question before you get back to your bacon and breakfast: Where did you learn all of this?"

"I have been a Mental Performance Mastery (MPM) Certified Coach for the last ten years. Everything that I have shared with you since we met, I got from the MPM Certification Course," Sunny answered. "Once you fill out your MVP Process, if you want more, that's your next step."

"Remember Mr. Big, the best investment you can make, is always an investment into yourself and into your mental health and mental performance. Mental performance is really the missing link in all of human performance. I know you will love it."

THE ONE PERCENT BETTER QUESTIONS FOR REFLECTION

This book was not written for you to read and then put on a shelf in your learner's library. This book was written to inspire you to take simple and consistent action over time to help you close the gap from where you are to where you want to be.

In my experience as an author, teacher, coach consultant and speaker, the best time for reflection is after reading something that moves you to take action.

Please use the following pages for reflection on what you have read in *this book* to help you close the gap from where you are to where you want to be.

QUESTION #1

Mr. Big's wife calls the alarm clock an "opportunity clock" because every day is "*an opportunity to have a positive impact on the lives of others and an opportunity to take a step towards the optimal version of you.*" **When you first hear the alarm clock chime its familiar tune each morning, what's your initial thought? (No judgment here, so go ahead and be brutally honest).**

QUESTION #2

From Day One of the new school year, Mr. Big's focus is on counting down the days until the next summer. **What is your #1 focus at the start of a school year?**

QUESTION #3

When he's forced to ride with his wife Erin to school, Mr. Big learns that she listens to The Mental Performance Daily Podcast and The Success Hotline Podcast each morning. The first morning they ride together, the message talks about the importance of "intention." Mr. Big says, *"My only intention was to survive the day and take off one more number on my list of days left in the school year."* **As you begin each day, what is your intention? What is the purpose you have in mind as you go into each new day?**

QUESTION #4

Sunny describes Mr. Big's wife Erin as someone who "brings the juice." **What does that mean? Do you bring "the juice" to your classroom each day? Why or why not?**

QUESTION #5

What's the difference between someone who is "interested" vs. "invested"? **Which one are you?**

QUESTION #6

In chapter 13, Sunny states, "What I have come to realize is that a great school year is simply a by-product of great weeks, and great weeks are a by-product of stacking great days on top of great days." **How could this approach of taking things one day—one moment—at a time affect the amount of energy and investment you bring each day?**

QUESTION #7

What is the significance of the numbers one percent and 14:24? **How can you use these numbers to begin improving yourself personally and professionally?**

QUESTION #8

In chapter 16, the message from Success Hotline that Mr. Big learns that day is that "change is inevitable; growth is optional." **In what areas could your reluctance to embrace change be negatively affecting your growth? When change occurs, do you get bitter, or do you embrace growth and find a way to get better?**

QUESTION #9

Often, when we try to make positive changes in our lives, our positive growth is only temporary—then we fall back into our old habits. **What is the key to moving from temporary to legendary that Sunny talks about in chapter 18?**

QUESTION #10

Often, we have all the ABILITY we need for personal and professional growth, but we are BLOCKING our ability by failing to implement a strategy to improve in a specific area. **What are a few areas where you'd like to improve personally and professionally, and what strategies could you use in your one percent better intention?**

QUESTION #11

What does the phrase *"in you before what you do"* that Sunny talks about in chapter 20 **mean to you?**

QUESTION #12

What are the three components of **The 3 Step Success Cycle?**

QUESTION #13

What are the four components of **The 4 Step Goal Formula?**

QUESTION #14

What's the difference between **happiness and fulfillment?**

QUESTION #15

What benefit does the **Daily Success Checklist or the *Habit Share* app provide?**

QUESTION #16

In chapter 23, Sunny asks Mr. Big, "Why don't you teach today like you are on a one-day contract and your performance determines if you get to come back or not?" **How would your attitude, energy, and intention change if you approached each day that way?**

QUESTION #17

What do each of the letters in the acronym **"MVP"** stand for?

QUESTION #18

Take some time to develop your own (14:24) one percent better intention and your own personal MVP process.

YOUR 14:24
ONE PERCENT BETTER INTENTION

YOUR MISSION

YOUR VISION

YOUR CORE PRINCIPLES

ABOUT THE AUTHOR

Brian Cain, MPM, is a #1 best-selling author, speaker and the creator of *The Mental Performance Daily Podcast, The 10 Pillars of Mental Performance Mastery (MPM) System, The MPM Coaches Certification Course* and *The 30 Days To MPM Athletes Program.*

It's his mission to certify 10,000 coaches who each educate, empower and energize more than 1,000 clients so that together they can impact and influence over 10,000,000 lives.

Brian has worked with coaches, athletes, and teams at the Olympic level and in the National Football League (NFL), National Basketball Association (NBA), National Hockey League (NHL), Ultimate Fighting Championship (UFC), on the Professional Golf Tour (PGA) and in Major League Baseball (MLB).

His client list includes 8 former UFC Champions, 4 Major League Baseball Cy Young Award winners, a Heisman Trophy winner and more than 1,000 professional sports draft pics including the #1 overall pick in both the MLB and NFL Draft.

A former high school teacher and administrator, Brian personally knows the challenges teachers and administrators battle on a daily basis to be their best.

Brian has spoken on stages all over the world and has delivered his keynote on getting *One Percent Better* at in-service trainings, corporate retreats, leadership summits, and conventions in education, sports and business.

Highly sought after as a speaker and trainer, Brian delivers his message with passion, in an engaging style that keeps his audiences energized, focused and empowered through the learning process.

As someone who lives what he teaches, Brian will inspire you and, more importantly, give you the tools necessary to get the most out of your career and life and close the gap from where you are to where you want to be by living with your own personal *One Percent Better Intention.*

START LISTENING TO
MENTAL PERFORMANCE DAILIY
PODCAST

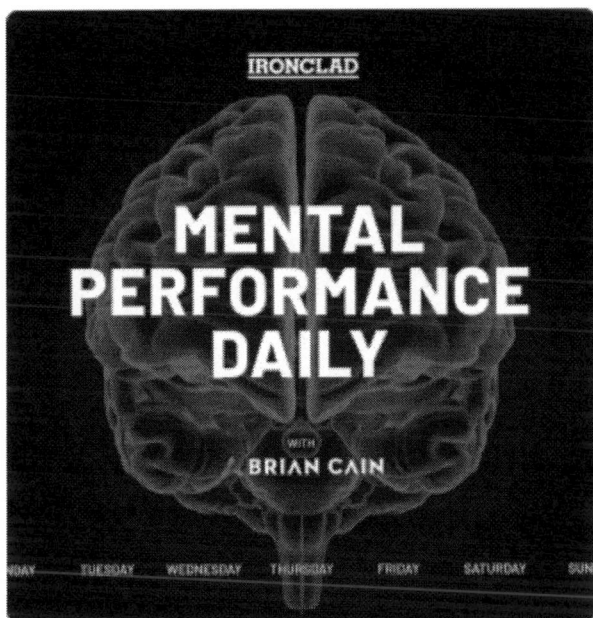

Want to receive the same mental performance strategies that Mr. Big and Erin listened to on the way to school every day. Now you can.

LISTEN TODAY AT
BrianCain.com

BECOME A
MENTAL PERFORMANCE MASTERY
(MPM) CERTIFIED COACH

Want to receive the same training, mentorship and certification that helped Sunny develop an elite mindset and unstoppable energy? Become a Brian Cain Mental Performance Mastery (MPM) Certified Coach and start teaching *The One Percent Better Intention* and *The 10 Pillars of Mental Performance Mastery* so you can help others close the gap from where they are to where they want to be.

JOIN THE INSIDERS LIST
TO SAVE $200 & LEARN MORE AT
BrianCain.com/certification

BECOME A
MENTAL PERFORMANCE MASTERY
(MPM) TRAINED ATHLETE

Want to receive the same mental performance training that Brian provides some of the greatest athletes on the planet? Develop the elite mindset, routines and habits of excellence you need to get the results you've been missing.

LEARN MORE AND JOIN
OTHER TOP ATHLETES AT
BrianCain.com/athletes

TEAM CONSULTING

Brian offers team consulting packages to help facilitate The One Percent Better approach in your team, school or corporation. Coupled with his *10 Pillars of Mental Performance Mastery System* and his world class experience as a consultant, let Brian help you close the gap from where are to where you want to be.

LEARN MORE AT
BrianCain.com/consulting

KEYNOTE SPEAKING

Brian delivers his message with energy, engagement, and enthusiasm to help educate, empower, and energize his audiences. If you are looking for a keynote speaker who will energize your team/staff and leave them with simple and powerful tools to transform their lives and the lives of those they lead, contact Brian today.

LEARN MORE AT
BrianCain.com/speaking

1-1 COACHING

Brian works one-on-one with teachers, students, coaches, athletes, and executives in applying *The one percent better intention* and *The 10 Pillars of Mental Performance Mastery.*

He is now offering one-on-one coaching opportunities where he can work with you directly to apply the information in this book to your life so that you can close the gap from where you are to where you want to be.

LEARN MORE AT
BrianCain.com/coaching

CONNECT WITH BRIAN

@BrianCainPeak

/BrianCainPeak

/BrianCainPeak

/BrianCainPeak

@BrianCainPeak

CONTACT BRIAN BY VISITING
BrianCain.com/contact

WHERE'S BRIAN?

Find out when Brian will be in your area and inquire about having him come speak with you and your team, school or organization!

VIEW BRIAN'S CALENDAR AT
BrianCain.com/calendar

Made in the USA
Columbia, SC
09 April 2025

2c880378-3de4-437e-a2e0-f4b1a71cebb9R01